# Life in the
# THIRTEEN COLONIES

# North Carolina

Richard Worth

**children's press**®
An imprint of
**SCHOLASTIC**

**Library of Congress Cataloging-in-Publication Data**

Worth, Richard.
 North Carolina / by Richard Worth.
  p. cm. — (Life in the thirteen colonies)
 Includes bibliographical references and index.
 ISBN 0-516-24576-7
 1. North Carolina—History—Colonial period, ca. 1600–1775—Juvenile literature. 2. North Carolina—History—1775–1865—Juvenile literature. I. Title. II. Series.
 F257.W75 2004
 975.6'02—dc22

2004007453

A Creative Media Applications Production
Design: Fabia Wargin Design
Production: Alan Barnett, Inc.
Editor: Matt Levine
Copy Editor: Laurie Lieb
Proofreader: Tania Bissell
Content Research: Lauren Thogersen
Photo Researcher: Annette Cyr
Content Consultant: David Silverman, Ph.D.

Photo Credits © 2004

Cover: Top left © Getty Images/Hulton Archive; Top right © North Wind Archives; Bottom left © Getty Images/Hulton Archive; Bottom right © North Wind Archives; Background © Bettmann/CORBIS; Title Page © North Wind Archives; p. 2 © North Wind Archives; p. 5 © Bettmann/CORBIS; p. 11 © North Wind Archives; p. 12 © North Wind Archives; p. 15 © North Wind Archives; p. 20 © North Wind Archives; p. 24 © North Wind Archives; p. 27 © North Wind Archives; p. 28 © North Wind Archives; p. 31 © North Wind Archives; p. 32 © Araldo de Luca/CORBIS; p. 34 © Michael Freeman/CORBIS; p. 36 © North Wind Archives; p. 39 © North Wind Archives; p. 42 © North Wind Archives; p. 47 © North Wind Archives; p. 48 © North Wind Archives; p. 52 © North Wind Archives; p. 54 © North Wind Archives; p. 56 © Bettmann/CORBIS; p. 58: Top left © Richard T. Nowitz/CORBIS; Top right © Bettmann/CORBIS; Bottom left © The Newberry Library; Bottom right © Royalty-Free/CORBIS; p. 59: Top left © Colonial Williamsburg Foundation; Top right © Bettmann/CORBIS; Bottom left © The Newberry Library; Bottom right © Colonial Williamsburg Foundation; p. 60 © North Wind Archives; p. 66 © North Wind Archives; p. 69 © North Wind Archives; p. 70 © North Wind Archives; p. 73 © North Wind Archives; p. 74 © North Wind Archives; p. 78 © Royalty-Free/CORBIS; p. 81 © Bettmann/CORBIS; p. 82 © Getty Images/Hulton Archive; p. 86 © North Wind Archives; p. 88 © North Wind Archives; p. 90 © North Wind Archives; p. 94 © North Wind Archives; p. 97 © North Wind Archives; p. 100 © North Wind Archives; p. 102 © North Wind Archives; p. 105 © North Wind Archives; p. 107 © North Wind Archives; p. 108 © North Wind Archives; p. 113 © Bettmann/CORBIS; p. 118: Top left © North Wind Archives; Top right © North Wind Archives; Bottom © North Wind Archives; p. 119: Top left © North Wind Archives; Top right © North Wind Archives; Bottom © North Wind Archives

# Contents

**THE ORIGINAL THIRTEEN COLONIES, 1775**

NEW FRANCE

MAINE
(part of Mass.)

St. Lawrence River

Lake Champlain

Lake Ontario

Lake Erie

Mohawk R.

NEW HAMPSHIRE

Falmouth

Portsmouth
Newburyport
Salem
Boston

MASSACHUSETTS

Cape Cod

Albany

NEW YORK

Connecticut River

Hudson R.

Hartford
New Haven

Newport

RHODE ISLAND
CONNECTICUT

Delaware R.

Susquehanna R.

Appalachian Mountains

New York
Perth Amboy

Long Island

PENNSYLVANIA

Pittsburgh

Philadelphia
York

Burlington

NEW JERSEY

New Castle

DELAWARE

Ohio River

Baltimore

Potomac R.

MARYLAND

Alexandria

James River

Richmond

Williamsburg

VIRGINIA

Norfolk

Chesapeake Bay

Atlantic Ocean

Roanoke River

Hillsboro

Halifax

Edenton

Salem

NORTH CAROLINA

Bath

Cape Hatteras

Salisbury

New Bern

Pamlico Sound

Charlotte

Cross Creek

Cape Fear R.

Camden

Wilmington

SOUTH CAROLINA

Augusta

Savannah River

Georgetown

GEORGIA

Charles Town

Savannah

SPANISH TERRITORY

NORTH
EAST
WEST
SOUTH

**Legend**

Colonial boundaries
(The western boundaries of many colonies were undefined in 1775.)

0          125          250

Scale in Miles

# A Nation Grows
## From Thirteen Colonies

North Carolina is located in the southeastern part of the United States. It is bordered by Virginia to the north and South Carolina to the south. Its eastern border is the Atlantic Ocean and to the west lie the Appalachian Mountains and Tennessee.

Native Americans lived along the coast and throughout the hills and mountains of North Carolina's interior. European explorers were in awe of the land's natural beauty and **abundant** wildlife. Their stories inspired many settlers to leave England for a new way of life in North Carolina.

The colonists of North Carolina had a strong interest in politics. Their beliefs contributed to the formation of the U. S. Constitution. North Carolina was one of the largest colonies, and its influence was felt throughout the period leading up to and after the War of Independence.

*The map shows the thirteen English colonies in 1775. The colored sections show the areas that were settled at that time.*

# CHAPTER ONE

# European Discovery

░░░░░░░░░░░░░░░░░░░░░░░░░░░░░░░

## First Explorers

In 1524, Francis I, the king of France, wanted to create a new empire in America. His rival, the king of Spain, had already claimed lands in this new world. Now King Francis wanted gold and other riches like the Spanish had found.

But the Spanish already had a head start. They had taken control of many islands in the Caribbean Sea. They had also taken Mexico from the powerful tribe that controlled it. Spanish soldiers had stolen the natives' land and taken vast riches in gold and silver.

The French king chose a brave Italian sea captain and pirate named Giovanni da Verrazano to go to America. His job was to claim land for France and to start a French empire in America.

*Giovanni da Verrazano sailed his ship more than 2,000 miles (3,200 kilometers) to reach the coast of North Carolina.*

Verrazano sailed his ship, *La Dauphine* (Dolphin), across the Atlantic Ocean from France to the shores of North America. After a journey of more than 2,000 miles (3,200 kilometers), he spotted land. Small islands dotted the coast, and lush forest stretched far inland. Verrazano had reached the coast of what would become the colony of North Carolina. He was the first European to visit this part of America.

The captain described the land as containing "faire fields and plains...good and wholesome aire." There were trees "greater and better than any in Europe" and a "great **bounty** of game and fowl of every kind."

Verrazano then sailed north as far as Nova Scotia, Canada, and was the first European to explore New York Harbor. Returning to France, he reported his findings to the king. The explorer felt that the land he had seen was the perfect place for a French colony. But before he could convince Francis I to send settlers, the Spanish began building a settlement there. The French king had been beaten by his Spanish rivals again.

The Spanish claimed all the territory that would become the states of Florida, Georgia, South Carolina, and North Carolina. They called the territory north of Florida Carolana, which means "land of Charles" in Latin. For the next sixty years, the Spanish and French tried to establish settlements in the region. They fought against each other off

# Corsairs

Giovanni da Verrazano was a corsair or pirate. Corsairs were sea captains who roamed the Mediterranean Sea and Atlantic Ocean searching for ships to attack. They would capture a ship and then take everything they found on board, including the possessions of the passengers and crew.

Although piracy was illegal, countries such as France and Spain sometimes protected pirates who attacked the countries' enemies. In 1520, Verrazano captured a Spanish treasure ship returning

*Verrazano's success as a pirate prepared him to captain a ship in search of the New World.*

from Mexico. This feat impressed the French king, Francis I, and sparked his interest in exploring America.

the Carolana coast, and they sent settlers to set up colonies. But it was difficult to build towns in the swampy territory, and the settlers also faced disease and hostile Indians. Neither country was able to overcome these problems. By the late 1500s, both countries gave up. The Spanish retreated to Florida and the Caribbean, and the French left the area completely.

# Early English Exploration

North Carolina remained unsettled and unexplored by Europeans. Then, in 1584, English sea captain Walter Raleigh sent two ships to North America. They were commanded by Philip Amadas and Arthur Barlowe. On July 4, Barlowe and Amadas reached what is today called the Outer Banks of North Carolina.

The two ships sailed through the chain of islands and sandbars that make up the Outer Banks. In Pamlico Sound, Amadas and Barlowe explored one of the islands, called

## Sailing West to the Far East

In addition to exploring America, Giovanni da Verrazano was searching for a new route to China, India, and Japan. Europeans called these countries the Far East. In the Far East, European explorers traded for many beautiful and unusual items, like fine silk and spices. The only way to reach the Far East from Europe was to sail around the tip of Africa. The journey took more than a year to complete and passed through very dangerous waters.

The people of the time believed that there was a water passage across North America that linked the Atlantic and Pacific Oceans. They called this mythical waterway the Northwest Passage. European sailors believed that it would provide a shorter route to the Far East. Many explorers searched for the Northwest Passage. They discovered many new lands in North and South America, but they never achieved their goal.

Roanoke by the local Indians. Barlowe wrote that the island was

*full of grapes...both on the sand and on*
*the greene soile on the hils...also [climbing near] the*
*tops of high Cedars, that I think in all*
*the world the like abundance is not to be found.*

Barlowe traded with some of the Native Americans who inhabited the island. He called them "very handsome and goodly people."

When Barlowe and Amadas returned to England, they told Walter Raleigh about their discovery of North Carolina and the Outer Banks. Soon more Europeans sailed to the region. Their arrival would transform the lives of the Native people who lived there.

## An English Visitor

European explorers and settlers met a variety of Indian tribes in North Carolina. Indians had been living on the coasts of North Carolina for centuries. These people belonged to a family of tribes called Algonquian. They included the Chowanoc, Roanoke, Secotan, and Croatan peoples. The Algonquian tribes all spoke the same language.

An English settler named Thomas Harriot, who had also been sent by Walter Raleigh, described the Indians he met on two trips to North Carolina in 1585 and 1587:

*They are a people clothed with loose*
*mantles [tunics] made of deer skins & aprons*
*of the same around about their middles....*
*And to confess a truth, I cannot remember*
*that ever I saw a better or quieter people.*

Harriot wrote detailed descriptions of the North Carolina Indians and their way of life. His journals, which were published in England, give a glimpse into the way the first English settlers viewed the natives.

When the English arrived in the 1580s, there were 7,000 Algonquian living in the region. One tribe, the

Chowanoc, numbered about 2,500 people living in eighteen villages. The English brought items for trade but they also brought diseases like measles and smallpox. The natives often became deathly ill after meeting Europeans for the first time. Within a few years after the English first landed in North Carolina, diseases had killed more than one-quarter of the Indian population.

Harriot wrote that

*a few days after our departure from every...*
*town, the people began to die very fast, and*
*many in short space.... The disease was so*
*strange, that they neither knew what it was,*
*nor how to cure it; the like by report of the oldest*
*men in the country never happened before.*

Neither the Indians nor the English fully understood what was happening. It was not known at the time that disease was caused by viruses and germs that people carry and spread to others. Europeans had developed immunity to these diseases, but Native Americans had not. The European newcomers in North Carolina and the other American colonies killed many thousands of Native Americans just by stepping foot into their villages.

# The Algonquian Way of Life

Before the Europeans came to North Carolina, the Algonquian peoples had lived there for hundreds of years. They lived together in large families, including grandparents, parents, and children. Their villages contained up to thirty rectangular houses made out of wooden poles covered by grass mats. The houses had arched roofs made from tree bark.

Most of the houses were small and had only one room. The tribal chief and his family, however, lived in a larger house with several rooms. Each village was surrounded by a wooden wall, called a **palisade**, to protect the people from dangerous animals and other Indian tribes.

Villages were set up near the fields where the Algonquian grew their crops. They grew several types of corn, which was harvested twice during the year. Along with the corn, the Indians planted beans. Nearby they planted pumpkins, squash, and tobacco. Men and women worked together in the fields, planting seeds and then weeding and harvesting the crops. One man in each village was assigned the task of keeping watch over the fields. He sat in a wooden chair and drove away any birds or animals that came to eat the plants.

Each year, the families of the tribe joined together for celebrations. For example, the green-corn festival was held to mark the harvest. These celebrations were filled with dancing and singing. The Algonquian also held religious

*A staple of the Indian diet was fish, plentiful in the streams, lakes, and rivers nearby.*

ceremonies, led by Indian priests. They prayed to a variety of gods. Statues of these gods were carved and carried into battle to protect the warriors. The Algonquian believed that a person who was killed after living a good and just life would enter another world in the afterlife and be rewarded.

The Indian diet consisted of a variety of fish and meat. The Indians fished from boats hollowed out of tree trunks. They used traps and nets to catch the fish. Sometimes, the Algonquian fished at night. They carried torches that attracted the fish to the surface of the water, where they were speared. The spears were made of reeds with pieces of crab shell used as the sharp points.

The Algonquian also hunted animals in the forests along the Carolina coast. They used bows made from the wood of maple trees and arrows carved from reeds. The arrowheads were made from shells or the teeth of large fish. Deer provided a steady source of meat for the Indians. Never wasteful, the Algonquian used the deerskin to make clothing and moccasins. Men fastened deerskin around their waists to form **loincloths**. Women wore dresses and cloaks of deerskin that were sometimes decorated with beads.

*Algonquian villages were organized around their planting fields.*

# Indians of the Carolina Interior

Many Native Americans also lived in the interior sections of Carolina. Their villages were located along the river valleys at the base of the Blue Ridge Mountains.

Among the interior tribes were the Tuscarora, who were related to the Iroquois of northern New York. According to Tuscarora legend, the Iroquois had once tried to cross a wide river by holding onto a grapevine. The vine broke after only part of the tribe had made it across the river. This group migrated to Carolina and became the Tuscarora, while the rest of the Iroquois remained behind in New York.

Like the Algonquian, the Tuscarora lived in domed, wooden houses surrounded by palisades. They also grew corn, beans, and squash. This grouping of vegetables was known as the "Three Sisters." These crops were planted together in mounds and each one helped the others grow better. The beans supplied nitrogen, a rich fertilizer, to the soil. The fertilizer made the other two plants grow stronger. The beans were climbing plants that grew up around the cornstalks, using them for support. The squash had broad leaves that shaded the other two plants and kept the soil moist.

One way the Tuscarora caught fish was to place an herb that was harmless to humans but deadly to fish in the water.

The dead or stunned fish would float to the surface, where they were easy to gather.

The Indians also hunted bears. They skinned these animals and used their thick coats to make warm garments for the winter. The Tuscarora also used bear grease on their hair and skin as an insect repellent in the summertime.

Among the Tuscarora, when a couple married, they went to live with the woman's family. Children were considered part of their mother's family, not their father's. Women also participated in making decisions that affected the entire tribe, including the selection of the Tuscarora chiefs.

To the west of the Tuscarora villages, the Catawba tribe lived along the river valleys. The name *Catawba* means "river people." The Catawba villages were similar to those of the other Native Americans in Carolina. The small, circular houses were built of wooden poles covered in bark. The roofs were made of cattails that grew in the streams. In the center of the village was an area for ceremonies and festivals. Villages also contained a large council house where the Catawba met to make important decisions about the tribe. Although the Catawba selected a chief, other tribe members had a say in important decisions. The villagers met regularly to express their opinions and decide what actions the chief should take.

# The Cherokee of the Mountains

The Cherokee lived along the Blue Ridge Mountains of western Carolina. They were the largest Indian tribe in the area. By the late 1500s, there were as many as 200 Cherokee villages in the area.

Each Cherokee village consisted of thirty to sixty houses. During the cold winter months, Cherokee families lived in cone-shaped homes with peaked roofs. In the summer, they built rectangular houses that were open-ended and much cooler. As in other Carolina tribes, grandparents, their children, and their grandchildren all lived together in one house.

Like men in the Tuscarora tribe, Cherokee men moved into the houses of their wives' families. Children became part of their mother's family and belonged to her clan—a large group consisting of many families related to each other.

*Some North Carolina tribes dried and preserved the bodies of their chiefs. This drawing of an Indian tomb in North Carolina was done by a European explorer in the 1500s.*

Cherokee families depended on food from the "Three Sisters." Women did the planting, weeding, and harvesting. They ground corn into meal and then made it into bread or used it in stews. Women also sewed the clothing worn by the Cherokee. Most clothes were made from deerskin. First, the skin was stripped from the deer and the hair was removed. The skin was softened with a mixture of animal brains and water. The skin was dried and then made into tunics, dresses, moccasins, or simple loincloths.

## Cherokee Entertainment

Despite the demands of hunting, fishing, farming, and raising families, the Native Americans of Carolina found time for recreation. They enjoyed a variety of competitions, including races and archery contests. The Indians would shoot arrows into stacks of corn to see whose arrow would go in the farthest. The winner was considered to be the strongest archer.

They also played a game with polished stone disks and spears. The Indians would roll the disks across a field and then throw their spears to the spot they thought the disk would stop. The player whose spear landed closest to the place where the disk stopped won points. The game gave young men practice in throwing spears, which was important for hunting. The spectators often bet on the outcome.

Women also participated in major decisions that were made in the Cherokee council house. Inside the council house, a sacred fire was kept burning throughout the year. Each November, at a New Year's celebration, the old fire was put out and a new one was lit.

# The Coming of the English

The traditional way of life that the Native Americans of Carolina had followed for centuries was drastically changed when the English arrived at the end of the sixteenth century. At first, the Indians welcomed the English and taught them how to plant corn and survive in the wilderness. This friendly attitude began to change when English settlers attacked the Indian villages. The settlers also expanded their homes and villages onto sacred Indian hunting grounds. As these settlements grew over the next two centuries, the conflicts between the Indians and the English would develop into full-scale, bloody wars.

NORTH
CAROLINA,
1775

MARYLAND

VIRGINIA

*Appalachian Mountains*

Great
Dismal
Swamp

*Roanoke River*

Guilford
Court
House

Hillsboro

Wachovia
Bethabara

Salem

Raleigh

*Neuse River*

*Deep R.*

Fort
Raleigh

*Tar River*

*Pamlico
River*

Bath

Catechna

NORTH CAROLINA

*Catawba River*

New Bern

*Pamlico Sound*

Ocracoke
Island

King's Mountain

*Pee Dee River*

*Lumber River*

*Broad River*

Brunswick

*Cape Fear River*

Moore's
Creek Bridge

Wilmington

SOUTH CAROLINA

GEORGIA

*Atlantic
Ocean*

NORTH

WEST

EAST

SOUTH

Legend

Colonial boundaries
(The western boundaries of many
colonies were undefined in 1775.)

0        50        100

Scale in Miles

# CHAPTER TWO

# The Lost Colonies

## Establishing the New Colony

When Barlowe and Amadas returned to England, they told Walter Raleigh about what they had seen. They described the forests filled with animals to hunt and the fertile land where Indians grew crops. The climate was much warmer and more pleasant than England's cold, damp weather. Raleigh was convinced. He decided that the island of Roanoke sounded like an excellent location for a new colony.

Raleigh organized a group of settlers to go to America and set up an English colony on Roanoke. He persuaded the queen of England, Elizabeth I, to help pay for the **expedition**. She granted Raleigh a royal **charter** that allowed him to settle the land in the name of the English government.

Raleigh chose his cousin, Sir Richard Grenville, to lead the band of settlers. Grenville's second-in-command was a man named Ralph Lane, who worked for Queen Elizabeth's government. Raleigh wanted to get an accurate description

*This map shows how North Carolina looked in 1775.*

of what the settlers found in the New World. To accomplish this, he sent an artist named John White on the journey to draw pictures of the Native Americans, animals, and countryside. The scientist Thomas Harriot was to write down everything he saw. His accounts became one of the first records of Indian life in the America.

Seven ships filled with supplies and a hundred male settlers left England in April 1585. They reached the Outer Banks in late June. As they approached the coast, a terrible storm arose. The ships survived but the settlers lost some of their supplies, including much of their food, in the storm. The sailors named the nearby point of land Cape Fear.

*Artists captured the landscapes of the New World and brought the drawings back to England.*

# Fort Raleigh

In July, the English colonists finally reached Roanoke Island. They quickly set up a village. They built a wooden **stronghold**, called Fort Raleigh, and placed small cannons around the fort. The new settlers did not know what to expect from the Indians on Roanoke.

Some of the settlers had no interest in establishing friendly relations with the Indians or building a colony. According to Thomas Harriot, many were interested only in looking for gold and "had little or no care for any other thing but to pamper their bellies," so that "lacking fair houses, dainty food, and soft beds, the country was to them miserable."

The colonists were not skilled farmers or hunters. Before the summer ended, they began to run low on food. After some discussion, Grenville decided to return to England for more supplies. He left Ralph Lane in charge of Fort Raleigh. This decision would doom the colony.

## The Lost Men

When the Roanoke colonists sailed back to England, they left between fifteen and eighteen men at Fort Raleigh. There is no record of why these men stayed behind. Perhaps they thought other colonists would someday return and they wanted to protect the fort. Whatever the reason, the men were never heard from again. These were the first English colonists to disappear at Roanoke. They would not be the last.

# The Roanoke Island Indians

Lane met with the local Indian leaders, and at first the Indians helped the colonists. They supplied the newcomers with corn and taught them how to catch fish. But Lane did not return their **hospitality**. Instead, he kidnapped Indians and forced them to give him information about the surrounding country. Over the next eight months, Lane and the other colonists quarreled and fought with the Indians. The Roanoke tribe feared that the colony was going to move onto their hunting grounds.

When Lane heard that the Roanoke chief, Wingina, planned to attack Fort Raleigh and massacre the settlers, he decided to strike first. In June 1586, a group of settlers led by Lane attacked Wingina's village at night, killing the chief.

When Lane returned to Fort Raleigh, he discovered that a large English expedition had arrived. This fleet of ships was led by Sir Francis Drake, an English explorer and sea captain. Although Drake had brought supplies, he offered Lane a ship if the settlers wanted to return to England. With no sign of Grenville's return, Lane and the colonists abandoned Fort Raleigh. He and his men boarded Drake's ships and returned to England.

Not long after the colonists left, Grenville returned from England with fresh supplies. He found no one at Fort

Raleigh and so he sailed back to England. The first English settlement in North Carolina had come to an end. The next English colony would come to be shrouded in mystery.

# The John White Colony

Although Roanoke colony had been abandoned, Sir Walter Raleigh remained eager to send another expedition to the New World. John White's colorful pictures of the North Carolina countryside and Thomas Harriot's writings made people in England excited about going to settle in the New World. Harriot wrote that "the country about this place is so fruitful and good, that England is not to be compared to it."

## A Published Record

The Roanoke colony was not a total failure. Ralph Lane sent Thomas Harriot and John White on several expeditions away from Roanoke Island. They recorded what they saw and created some of the first maps of America.

In 1588, Harriot's detailed notes and White's beautiful drawings of the plants, animals, and native peoples of North Carolina and the surrounding region were published in a book titled *A briefe and true report of the new found land of Virginia*. Raleigh had named the whole region Virginia. This would become the name of the colony the English would establish north of Roanoke and the Outer Banks.

Raleigh convinced a group of wealthy merchants to form a company to sponsor a new colony. This time, John White would be the leader and governor of the new colony. It would be known as the John White Colony. Approximately 110 settlers signed up to accompany White. Each settler was promised 500 acres (200 hectares) to farm.

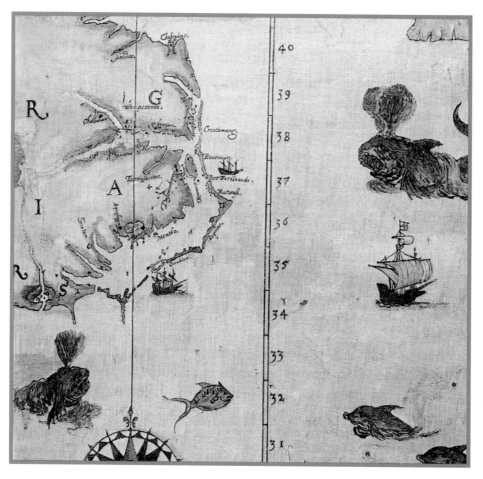

*John White drew this map of the Atlantic coast of North Carolina and Virginia on his first voyage to Virginia in 1585.*

White believed so strongly in the new colony that he brought along his daughter, Eleanor White Dare, and her husband, Ananias Dare, a bricklayer. Eleanor was expecting a baby but she and her husband decided to make the trip anyway.

On May 8, 1587, three ships carrying the settlers left Plymouth, England. After more than two months at sea, the colonists arrived at the Outer Banks on July 22. They set to work building the John White Colony at once.

On August 18, 1587, White's daughter gave birth to a girl. Her parents named her Virginia. She was the first English child born in North America. The joy of her birth, however, was overshadowed by a serious lack of food in the colony. The colonists had arrived in midsummer, which was too late in the season to plant, grow, and harvest enough corn to last through the winter.

The settlers asked White to return to England to obtain more supplies. At first, White wanted to send someone else. As the leader of the expedition, he felt it was his duty to remain in the colony. But the settlers insisted that he make the journey, so White finally agreed to go.

White knew that the fate of the colonists, including his daughter and new granddaughter, depended on a speedy journey to England and back. Unfortunately, for White and the colonists, a great war would prevent him from returning for almost three years.

# White's Return

Soon after White arrived home, Spain attacked England with 130 warships carrying 30,000 soldiers. This force was called the Spanish Armada. Every English ship in the nation, including White's, was needed to fight against the Spanish fleet. The English were badly outnumbered, but their ships were faster and easier to steer. The English used explosives to create great fires aboard their ships. Bravely, they sailed the burning ships into the Spanish fleet. This tactic caused the Spanish sea captains to panic. The English were able to control the fires on their own ships and sink many Spanish ships. The Spanish were beaten and sailed their remaining ships for home.

The battle of the Spanish Armada delayed White's return to Roanoke by almost three years. White set sail for the return journey to North Carolina in 1590, hoping he would not be too late. As he approached Roanoke, White saw smoke on the island. He hoped this meant that the colonists were welcoming him. But when he landed, White found no one. The colonists' houses were gone. Instead, he discovered footprints in the sand. He also found the letters CRO carved on the bark of a tree.

Before heading for England, White had instructed the colonists to leave behind some sign of where they were going if they were forced to leave Roanoke. The letters CRO

*Members of the John White Colony carved the word* Croatoan *onto a tree to let others know where they had moved.*

led him to believe that they had gone to the nearby island of Croatoan. On another tree near Fort Raleigh, he found the word CROATOAN. This confirmed his belief.

White desperately wanted to go to Croatoan, but heavy storms arose, and he was unable to sail there. He was finally forced to return to England without discovering what had become of the lost colony and his family. White never returned to the New World.

Historians have been puzzled for centuries over what happened to the John White Colony. Some believe that the colonists were killed by Indians. Others think they may have gone to live with the Croatoan Indians when their food ran out. Hurricanes, drought, and food shortages are all possible causes of their disappearance. The colonists' fate remains a mystery even today.

# CHAPTER THREE

# The Development of the New Colony

## Successful English Colonies

Following the failure of the Roanoke colony, the English waited almost two decades before trying to establish another colony in North Carolina. In 1607, England sent colonists to Jamestown in Virginia, not far north of the Outer Banks. This became the first permanent English colony in America.

By the 1650s, an estimated 22,000 settlers were living in Jamestown. As Jamestown got more crowded, some of its residents moved south to an area they called South Virginia. This was actually in the part of North Carolina known as

◁ *Colonists brought their way of life with them to the New World, including observing religious traditions.*

Albemarle. They established farms and traded with the Indians but did not build a permanent town.

An early description of Albemarle tells of the variety of wildlife available for settlers to hunt:

*deer in abundance, bigger and better meat than*
*ours in England.... Elkes of a large size, admirable*
*meat.... Beasts of prey, that are profitable for their*
*Furres, as Bevers, Otters, Foxes, Martins...fowle*
*of all sorts, Partridges and wild Turkies 100 in*
*a flock, some of the Turkies weighing 40 pounds,*
*Fish there are in great abundance, of all sorts.*

## A Charter to Settle Carolina

In 1660, Charles II became king of England. He changed the name of Carolana to Carolina and, as a reward for helping him claim power, gave a land grant to eight men. The grant included all of the present-day states of North Carolina, South Carolina, and Georgia. The eight men were called **proprietors**. The proprietors were given the power to collect taxes, hire an army, build forts, establish towns, and appoint governors. However, they were also supposed to include the settlers in making decisions and running the colony.

*Early settlers of Albemarle built towns and villages and traded with the Native Americans living there.*

The proprietors set up three separate **counties** in northern Carolina. The county of Albemarle was closest to Virginia. Clarendon was in the central area and Craven was in the south. The three counties would eventually become the colony of North Carolina. The remainder of the Carolina colony would eventually become the colonies of South Carolina and Georgia.

The proprietors appointed a governor for the entire colony of Carolina. They also elected an assembly to help

*North Carolina's forests were abundant with game for hunting.*

the governor. In addition, each of the North Carolina counties had its own governor and assembly. These county governments were controlled by the proprietors. Albemarle County would play the most important role in the history of North Carolina.

Before the counties could be established, the proprietors felt they needed to learn more about the area. In 1662, they hired Captain William Hilton of Barbados to explore the Carolina coast for them. His journey took him as far north as the Cape Fear River in present-day North Carolina. Hilton reported that he found "as good tracts of land, dry, well wooded, pleasant and delightful as we have seen any where in the world...with abundance of Deer and Turkies every where."

## North Carolina's First Settlers

Historians believe that Nathaniel Batts may have been the first permanent settler of North Carolina. Born about 1620, Batts was a fur trader. He was sent to Carolina about 1654 by a planter named Francis Yeardley to begin trading with the local Indians. Batts married Mary Woodhouse in 1656. They purchased land from the Indians on Albemarle Sound and established a homestead there.

Hilton's account was sent back to England and used to persuade people to come to the New World and settle in Carolina. Two years later, the proprietors selected governors for the Carolina colonies. William Drummond, a Virginia merchant, was selected to govern Albemarle.

Until 1689, Albemarle was the only North Carolina county with its own governor. The governor of Albemarle was considered an assistant to the governor of Carolina. Because Albemarle was close to the colony of Virginia, the proprietors wanted to maintain good trade relations with that colony. Therefore, they selected a man from Virginia as the first governor of Albemarle. They hoped this choice would help maintain order and improve trade with Virginia.

## No Nails and No Glass

Metal nails were very rare in the New World. Most backcountry settlers could not afford them and, even if they could, nails were very heavy to carry cross-country. Instead, most settlers' houses were built with wooden pegs. The pegs were shaped from tree branches and hammered into holes drilled into two pieces of wood to join them together.

Glass was also very rare on North Carolina farms. It was too fragile to be carted across rough back-country roads. Instead, settlers

*The first settlers built simple log cabins out of rough-hewn logs fit together with wooden pegs.*

used greased paper to cover windows. This let in some light and kept out the bugs. Many settlers' houses simply had open windows with shutters that were closed at night or when the weather turned cold or rainy.

# Persuading Settlers

Persuading settlers to leave the comforts of home in England for the unknown wilderness of Carolina was no easy task. The proprietors decided to publish books, pamphlets, and newspaper articles about the new colony.

In 1666, one of the proprietors, Robert Horne, published a glowing description of Carolina. Horne had never actually been to the colony, but that did not stop him from describing the many types of trees, great variety of wildlife, and wonderful climate there. "The Summer is not too hot," he said, "and the Winter is very short and moderate."

Even after reading about what a wonderful place Carolina was, many colonists preferred to settle in Virginia, because it was already an established colony. Virginia had many successful tobacco plantations, as well as cheap land. The yearly rents there were only one farthing, or one-quarter of a penny, per acre. To make the rent payment even easier, the rent could be paid in crops that farmers grew on their land.

The rents in Carolina were twice as much as those in Virginia and had to be paid in cash. So the proprietors drew up a document called the Great Deed of Grant in 1668. This made the rents in Carolina the same as they were in Virginia. As a result, more settlers came to the colony to establish farms.

# The Fundamental Constitutions

The arrival of settlers meant that the colony needed a government. The first plan for a government in Carolina was called the Fundamental Constitutions of Carolina. It was written in 1669 by Anthony Ashley Cooper, one of the proprietors.

*When word spread of the beauty of North Carolina, many settlers arrived with their families to begin a new life.*

According to the Fundamental Constitutions, the colony would be run by a governor. The governor would appoint a Grand Council to give help and advice. In addition, an elected **parliament** or assembly would be made up of farmers who owned at least 500 acres (200 hectares) of land. The members of this assembly paid the governor's salary. This gave them a lot of power over the governor.

The new constitution also called for religious tolerance in the colony. This was an unusual idea at the time. Many European countries allowed only one religion to be practiced. Spain, for example, was a Catholic country that did not permit Protestants or Jews to live there. Religious acceptance in Carolina was designed to attract settlers from Europe who wished to practice their own religions freely.

## The Growth of North Carolina

During the 1670s, more colonists began arriving in Carolina. Most of them settled in the southern part of the colony away from the three North Carolina counties. In 1680, Charles Town was settled on the Ashley River in what would become South Carolina. Charles Town would become the largest city in Carolina and one of the most important cities in the southern colonies. But this settlement was far from North Carolina.

In the north, Albemarle and the other counties grew much more slowly than Charles Town. Some settlers continued to drift south from Virginia. They built cabins, grew corn and tobacco, and raised farm animals. But Albemarle lacked a good harbor, so it wasn't easy to ship products to other colonies or other countries. Navigating through the Outer Banks was very tricky for a sailing ship. Inside the banks, the water was shallow and filled with shifting sandbars. Large ships could not enter the area.

As a result, North Carolina tobacco growers brought their crops to port towns in Virginia, where they were loaded on ships. Sometimes, small ships from New England that could navigate the Outer Banks picked up Carolina tobacco and shipped it to other North American colonies. But trade grew slowly in North Carolina because it had no deep-water harbor.

Then, England decided to make laws about trade, too. Parliament passed the Navigation Act of 1660. This act said that products produced by the colonists could be sold only in England. In addition, the products had to be sent there on English ships. The law also allowed English merchants to set the price they would pay for Carolina's tobacco. Carolina tobacco growers tried to get around this law by illegally selling their tobacco to New England merchants. These merchants transported it to other North American colonies or sold it to countries in Europe.

*Tobacco was a valuable crop, prompting the English king to impose
taxes on the colonists' earnings.*

So in 1673, the English Parliament passed a new law called the Plantation Duty Act. This required tobacco growers to pay a tax on any crop that was being shipped between colonies. These taxes made the colonists angry, and they often tried to avoid paying the taxes. The colonists sold their crops to smugglers who took them to other colonies and other countries without paying the English taxes.

## Political Turmoil in Albemarle

A protest over these taxes in Albemarle led to arguments and bloodshed. The protest was led by two of Albemarle's political leaders, John Jenkins and George Durant. Durant and Jenkins were successful tobacco growers who believed that the plantation duties were unfair.

Jenkins was named governor of Albemarle by the proprietors and then decided not to collect the plantation duties. This benefited the tobacco growers, most of whom were his friends. But the proprietors who wanted the tax money were outraged. They appointed a new governor named Thomas Miller to collect the taxes.

In 1677, when Miller tried to collect the tobacco tax, some of the settlers launched a **rebellion** to overturn Miller's government. This revolt, led by a man named John Culpeper, became known as Culpeper's Rebellion. Culpeper's followers armed themselves, stormed the governor's residence, and arrested Miller.

By 1689, the proprietors decided they needed a better way to control the three counties. They decided to unite all three counties under one government and called the area North Carolina. They appointed one governor and allowed the colonists to elect one assembly to run the three counties. The governor of North Carolina was a deputy governor under the governor of Carolina Colony, which included North Carolina, South Carolina, and Georgia.

The new government would help North Carolina to grow during the next decades.

# CHAPTER FOUR

# The Growth of North Carolina

## Religious Groups

Over the course of the eighteenth century, North Carolina continued to attract new settlers. Many came to the colony because of the religious freedoms offered under the Fundamental Constitutions.

In 1703, a Christian missionary named John Blair was sent to North Carolina to bring the Anglican religion to colonial settlers. Anglicanism was a type of Protestant religion that had been started in England during the sixteenth century. It was the main religion of England. The Anglican Church was supported by taxes paid by the English people and was called the Church of England. The proprietors of North Carolina wanted Anglicanism to be the established

*At the king's request, John Blair was sent to North Carolina to convert the colonial settlers to Anglicanism.*

religion of their colony also. However, following the terms of the Fundamental Constitutions, they were willing to allow other religious groups to remain in North Carolina. These included Presbyterians and Quakers.

When Blair arrived in the colony, he found very few religious Anglicans.

*The country may be divided into four sorts of people. First, the Quakers, who are the most powerful enemies to [the Anglican] Church.... The second sort are a great many who have no religion.... A third sort are something like Presbyterians.... A fourth sort, who are really zealous for the interest of the Church, are the fewest in number, but the better sort of people.*

## Religious War in North Carolina

In 1703, a new law was passed requiring all settlers to swear an **oath** of loyalty to the Anglican Church. Because this law went against the Fundamental Constitutions, the Quakers opposed it. The new governor, Thomas Cary, insisted that everyone obey it.

# Quakers

The Society of Friends was founded in England during the 1600s by George Fox. Members of this society were called Quakers by those who made fun of their religious beliefs. Quakers believed that they should bow down and tremble, or quake, before the Lord.

The Quakers taught that each person could find God by discovering the "inward light" within his or her own heart. Therefore, no clergy was necessary for their worship. The Quakers also opposed warfare and refused to pay taxes to support an established church.

Many Quakers left England and came to America during the seventeenth and eighteenth centuries. They settled in Rhode Island, a colony that guaranteed religious freedom. Pennsylvania, which was founded by the Quaker William Penn in the 1680s, also became home to many Quaker settlers. Others went to North Carolina, where religious tolerance was guaranteed under the Fundamental Constitutions. There, they established farms, entered politics, and became members of the North Carolina Assembly. The Quakers strongly opposed any laws that would force them to provide financial support to the Anglican Church.

The Quaker religion did not allow its members to swear oaths of any kind. An oath to the Anglican Church would require Quakers to say they would be loyal to that religion and not their own. This was one issue that had made Quakers leave England and settle in America. It took away their religious freedom. They refused to take the oath.

In 1707, the Quakers sent a representative to London, the capital of England, to demand that the proprietors **repeal** the law. Thinking that Governor Cary might have been too harsh, the proprietors removed him from office. They replaced him with William Glover. But Glover surprised the proprietors. He was even stricter about making sure people followed the new law. The Quakers decided that they might have been better off with Cary. Seeking the Quakers' support, Cary changed his mind about the oath. When Glover lost the election, Cary became governor again. This time, he ran the colony with the help of the Quakers. He refused to enforce the law supporting the Anglican Church in North Carolina.

## Cary's Rebellion

In 1711, a new governor, named Edward Hyde, came to North Carolina. Governor Hyde believed that all settlers should swear an oath of allegiance to the Anglican Church. Cary and his supporters refused to go along with this decision. Hyde considered them rebels who needed to be taught a lesson.

In the spring of 1711, Hyde gathered together about eighty armed men, who marched toward Cary's home. Cary knew this attack had been planned so he had already moved to a nearby fort. Behind the fort's walls, Cary had about forty men who were determined to stop Hyde. Reaching Cary's fort, Hyde realized that he could not possibly win this battle, so he and his men returned home.

Cary decided that he, not Hyde, should again be the governor of North Carolina. At the end of June, Cary attacked Hyde's forces. He was beaten back when Hyde received reinforcements—more soldiers from British ships stationed in Chesapeake Bay. After this defeat, Cary's forces fled, and his rebellion ended.

*British troops stationed on ships in Chesapeake Bay came to Governor Hyde's aid. They helped him defeat the rebels led by former governor Thomas Cary.*

*Boundaries were laid for new towns as settlers from other parts of Europe moved into North Carolina.*

# New Settlers

The battle over religion had not stopped new settlers from coming into North Carolina. For many, the colony still seemed like a better place to live than Europe. In France, King Louis XIV had forbidden Protestants called Huguenots from practicing their religion. As a result, many Huguenots fled to North America.

The Huguenots first arrived in Virginia, but much of the fertile land there had already been claimed by earlier settlers. The Huguenots then journeyed south to North Carolina, where many settled around the Pamlico River.

Around 1704, John Lawson, the **surveyor-general** of the colony, laid out the boundaries for the first town in North Carolina. The town, called Bath, was set up near the Pamlico River. By 1708, Bath had grown to include twelve houses and about fifty settlers, mainly Huguenots. Many of them traded with the Indians for furs. Others grew tobacco.

In 1710, a group of farmers from Switzerland and Germany came to North Carolina. Lawson found them a site to settle near the Neuse and Trent rivers. When their leader, Baron Christoph von Graffenried, arrived soon afterward, he helped the colonists build homes at the settlement. The town was named New Bern, after the city of Bern in Switzerland.

# War With the Tuscarora

The Tuscarora Indians saw the establishment of New Bern as harmful to their hunting grounds. This use of Tuscarora land angered the Indians. Since arriving in North Carolina, settlers had traded with the Indians for deerskins and furs. The colonists always tried to pay the Indians as little as possible for the valuable skins. In addition, settlers who actually bought lands from the Indians often refused to pay the agreed-upon prices.

The Indians were furious about something else the colonists did. The settlers kidnapped Indians and sold them as slaves. These Indian slaves were made to work on North Carolina's tobacco plantations. Sometimes they were sold to other colonies or shipped to the Caribbean, where they were put to work on sugar plantations. At first, the Tuscarora did little about this mistreatment. As John Lawson put it, "They are really better to us than we have been to them."

Then, in September 1711, Lawson and von Graffenried traveled along the Neuse River valley to explore the area. During their trip, they were captured by a band of Tuscarora and taken to the Indian town of Catechna. There, Lawson was killed by the Tuscarora. Graffenried was freed, but only after he promised that New Bern would not take part in the coming war with the Tuscarora. The Indians boldly told him they were planning to attack the settlers.

On September 22, the Tuscarora led a fierce attack on the North Carolina settlements. An estimated 500 Indian warriors burned houses and killed settlers. According to an eyewitness report,

> *The family of one Mr. Nevill was treated after this manner: the old gentleman himself, after being shot, was laid on the house-floor, with a clean pillow under his head.... A son of his was laid out in the yard, with a pillow laid under his head.... The master of the next house was shot and his body laid flat upon his wife's grave. Women were laid on their house-floors and great stakes run...through their bodies.*

Governor Hyde did not have enough soldiers to stop the Indians, so he called on South Carolina for help. That colony sent Colonel John Barnwell with a force of colonial militia (regular citizens who served as soldiers) and Yamasee Indians.

Barnwell's forces defeated the Tuscarora early in 1712. Barnwell burned their villages and destroyed their crops. Then he traveled to the Indian town of Catechna, where the Tuscarora were holding a group of colonists hostage. As

*North Carolina settlers fought the Tuscarora for control of the Indians' land.*

Barnwell's men attacked, the Tuscarora began to harm some of the hostages. Barnwell refused to call off his troops until the Tuscarora agreed to release the prisoners. At that point, Barnwell's army retreated.

But the war was not over. In April, the settlers attacked the Tuscarora again. This time, the Indians signed a peace treaty. They agreed to remain within a certain area in North Carolina. They were not allowed to build any forts on their lands. In return, they were to be left in peace.

Shortly afterward, the settlers broke their word. Once again, Indians were kidnapped and sold into slavery. This betrayal outraged the Tuscarora even more than before. They attacked more farms and villages.

On March 25, 1713, the Tuscarora were defeated by a combined force of Indians and settlers under the command of Colonel James Moore. Many Tuscarora braves were killed. As a result of this crushing defeat, the tribe left North Carolina and headed north to New York, where they lived among the Iroquois.

# Dealing With Pirates

The Tuscarora War and Cary's Rebellion had created a great deal of fear in North Carolina. Settlers were killed; homes and fields were destroyed. During the decade after the Tuscarora War, settlers worked hard to rebuild their towns and farms. As they rebuilt, they faced another threat—pirates.

At first, the colonists had a good, profitable relationship with the pirates. Many of these seamen had been **privateers** who owned private ships that they hired out to nations during times of war. Frequently, the privateers had brought the goods captured during wartime to North Carolina, where they sold the goods to the settlers for less than they paid for similar English products.

*Pirates spent most of the gold and other treasure they captured. But many people believe that some of their treasure may have been buried along the Outer Banks.*

When the Tuscarora War ended, some of the privateers decided that robbing merchant ships was an easy way to make money. So the privateers became pirates. They first operated in the Caribbean Sea, but they soon moved to the southern coast of North America. The Outer Banks of North Carolina provided them with protection. They could easily escape into the inlets along the coast and hide from the English warships trying to stop them.

# Blackbeard

One of the most well-known pirates of the time was Edward Teach. A successful privateer, Teach captured a French warship and named it *Queen Anne's Revenge*. Armed with forty cannons, the *Queen Anne's Revenge* became Teach's pirate ship. When a British warship was sent to stop him, Teach and his pirate crew defeated it.

Teach became known as Blackbeard the pirate. He made himself look scarier by braiding his long black beard and tying it in ribbons. Under his hat, he placed small pieces of rope. He burned these during battle so it appeared that smoke was coming out of his ears. Blackbeard was known as a fierce fighter who carried several pistols and knives. Reports of his violent behavior spread through the colonies.

In 1718, Blackbeard terrorized Charles Town's harbor in South Carolina, stopping merchant ships and taking prisoners. When his crew needed medicine, he demanded that the governor turn over what he wanted or he would kill his prisoners. The governor did exactly what Blackbeard ordered him to do.

Blackbeard and his crew then sailed for North Carolina. Governor Charles Eden said that Blackbeard could stay and live in Bath, but he had to give up piracy. If he chose to stay, his past crimes would be forgiven. Blackbeard accepted the deal and lived in Bath for a short time.

But Blackbeard's quiet life in Bath did not last very long. By the middle of 1718, he began attacking colonial merchant ships again. Since Eden seemed unable to stop him, Governor Alexander Spotswood of Virginia decided to take action. He sent out two ships under the command of Lieutenant Robert Maynard to find and kill Blackbeard.

*The pirate Blackbeard was finally defeated in a bloody battle with English troops sent by the governor of Virginia.*

Maynard caught up with the pirate at Ocracoke Island on November 21, 1718. Maynard ordered his men to hide below the top deck of his own ship and wait for Blackbeard to board. The pirate believed that Maynard was preparing to surrender. When Blackbeard boarded the ship, Maynard ordered his men to attack. The bloody struggle that followed came to an end when Blackbeard's head was cut off and hung from the mast of Maynard's ship.

About the same time as Blackbeard's death, other pirates in the area were captured also. It became clear to the pirates that North Carolina was no longer a safe harbor for them. With an end to piracy and the defeat of the Tuscarora, North Carolina was ready to expand again. New settlers came from Europe, new towns sprang up, and trade increased in newly safe harbors.

Teaching reading and writing to boys and girls was important to colonists, whose various religions valued education. Here are some common examples of items used by colonists who could read and write.

☛ *People who did not know how to read were given this book, or primer, to study.*

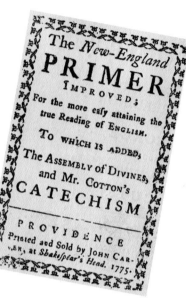

The *New-England* PRIMER IMPROVED; For the more easy attaining the true Reading of ENGLISH. To WHICH IS ADDED, The ASSEMBLY of DIVINES, and Mr. COTTON's CATECHISM PROVIDENCE Printed and Sold by JOHN CAR- ER, at Shakespear's Head. 1775.

✒ *Colonists used English stamps for their letters. Each stamp was worth three or four shillings and featured beautiful penmanship and etchings.*

✒ *Writing instruments, called quills, were fashioned from feathers sharpened at the end and then dipped into inkwells.*

✒ *Paddles, called hornbooks, that illustrated the alphabet were used at home and in school. The paper was covered with a thin layer of cow's horn to protect it.*

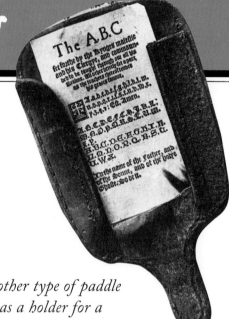

✍ *Writing desks were common in most homes, since letters were the only form of communication with those who lived far away.*

✍ *Another type of paddle served as a holder for a variety of lessons and papers.*

☞ *This printed illustration of the alphabet left out the letter V.*

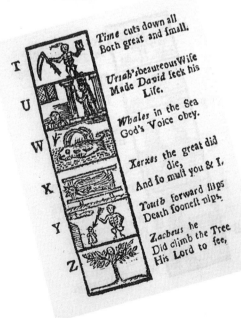

✍ *To print anything, metal stamps with letters were lined up to form words and sentences in a long and slow process.*

# CHAPTER FIVE

# Life in 18th-Century North Carolina

## A New Government

During the 1720s, England took control of North Carolina's government away from the proprietors. England was disappointed by North Carolina's small population. The low rents did not provide enough money for the English government. England believed that the Indian and pirate attacks scared away new settlers. It was also unhappy because so few colonists had joined the Anglican Church. Finally, England was angry with North Carolina's merchants for refusing to pay their plantation duties.

In 1712, North and South Carolina were split into two colonies. The English government paid the proprietors for their land in 1729, and North Carolina became a royal colony.

*The skirmishes with pirates and Native Americans led England to take control of North Carolina and claim it as a royal colony.*

England would now directly appoint a governor for North Carolina, and the English army and navy would protect the colony. The English encouraged more people to settle in North Carolina. The colony's population grew from 30,000 to 120,000 over the next thirty-five years.

# New Immigrants

Many of these new settlers came from Europe and began farming along the Cape Fear River. New towns were established at New Brunswick and Wilmington, both of which quickly became important ports.

## Community Meals

Most colonial drinking cups were made from wood or animal horns. Many of these large cups could hold more than a quart of liquid. Families would pass them around the table so that everyone could take a drink.

Instead of having individual plates at the supper table, many colonial families ate from a trencher. This was a large wooden block with a hollowed-out area in the center. The main dish was placed in the trencher and everyone ate from it.

In some households, children had to wait until their parents were finished before they ate. Children were expected to eat in silence.

Among the new immigrants in North Carolina were Scots from the highlands of Scotland. They left very poor farms in their homeland to settle in the rich farmland of North Carolina. The Scotch-Irish, who had originally migrated from Scotland to Ireland also came to escape bad harvests in Ireland, where many people were starving. Germany sent its share of immigrants to North Carolina as well. They were looking for a place where they could practice their religion freely. They established settlements at Wachovia, Bethabara, and Salem during the 1750s and 1760s.

# Farming in North Carolina

Most settlers in North Carolina became farmers. Farmers produced a variety of agricultural products, including corn, wheat, and peas. They also raised cows, horses, pigs, and other livestock. One of the most popular meals in the North Carolina colony was ham and hominy. Hominy was the dried and peeled kernels of corn that were ground up and made into mush or bread. **Surplus** hogs were slaughtered for shipment to England. Farmers also grew the plants hemp and flax. Hemp was made into rope, and flax was spun into linen for clothing.

# The People of North Carolina

Most European settlers who moved to America were poor farmers, **indentured servants**, and orphans. Others were members of the middle class. These included small farmers, store owners, and craftsmen such as blacksmiths and carpenters. A very few settlers belonged to the aristocracy, or upper class. These people owned large amounts of land. Most were owners of tobacco plantations. Plantation owners lived in huge homes with high ceilings, large glass windows, and many rooms. They imported much of their furniture, along with their dishes, glassware, and silverware, from England. They dressed in expensive clothes to show off their wealth and put on fancy parties at their homes for other members of the upper class. The upper class enjoyed dancing, as well as raising fine thoroughbred horses and racing them on tracks near their estates.

## The Middle Class

North Carolina's middle class lived along the rivers and in the backcountry. They built simple, wooden homes with one or two rooms on the ground floor. A cramped second floor usually had a loft where adults and children slept. For windows, the farmers cut openings in the sides of their homes that were left open in summer and closed with shutters in the winter. The houses contained simple, handmade furniture, including wooden beds, stools, and a few chairs.

Farm families were frequently large. As soon as they were old enough, children helped their parents on the farms. Everyone in the family worked tilling fields, planting crops, and bringing in the harvests. Girls also helped their mothers **spinning** flax into yarn and thread, cooking, sewing, and tending the vegetable gardens that were planted outside every home. There was little time for outside education, so reading and writing were taught at home.

## Education

In the small towns of North Carolina, there were very few schools for young people to attend. Rich planters and merchants hired tutors to teach their children at home. The families hoped that their children could one day go to college in England.

Middle-class children were often taught to read and write by their parents. The boys also learned trades through apprenticeships with craftsmen, such as carpenters or blacksmiths. Such apprenticeships, which were arranged by a boy's parents, lasted for seven years. At that point, a young apprentice who showed skill might open his own shop. Most girls remained at home and did not attend school. They were taught the skills necessary to raise families—cooking, spinning, sewing, and child care.

# The Lower Class

Indentured servants and poor farmers made up the lowest class. In colonial times, these people were called the "meaner sort." The word *mean* had a different definition than it does now. They were considered "low in value," not "unkind."

*In addition to tobacco, slaves planted crops of rice on plantations throughout North Carolina.*

Indentured servants agreed to work for farmers or craftsmen for a certain period of time (usually seven years). In exchange, the master paid for the servant's voyage to the New World. When the seven years were up, the indentured servant was free and often bought a farm or practiced a trade.

# Slavery

Among the many residents of North Carolina in the eighteenth century were African-American slaves. Settlers who came to the colony from Virginia and South Carolina brought their slaves with them. As early as 1712, there were about 800 slaves in North Carolina. By 1755, there were 19,000. Slaves made up only 20 percent of the entire population in North Carolina. In neighboring South Carolina, slaves outnumbered the white settlers.

Slaves had lived in America since the sixteenth century. The early Spanish settlers had relied on Indian slaves to work on their plantations in the New World. The Indians rapidly died off from European diseases such as smallpox and measles. To replace them, the Spanish imported slaves from Africa.

These slaves were kidnapped, chained together, and marched in front of white settlers to be sold. Others were sold into slavery in Africa as a punishment for committing crimes, like theft. Still others were captured during wars between African tribes. These tribes sold their captives to European slave traders.

# The Middle Passage

Slaves were brought to trading posts along Africa's west coast. There they were branded with a hot iron to show which trading company they belonged to. They were then loaded onto ships for the trip across the Atlantic Ocean to America. This voyage was called the Middle Passage.

On the slave ships, hundreds of slaves were packed together in a small area under the main deck. They were forced to live in unsanitary conditions with little air. Many of them died on the voyage across the Atlantic. When they were brought on deck during the day to eat, some Africans jumped overboard. They chose to drown, rather than spend their lives in slavery.

When they arrived at an American port such as Charles Town, South Carolina, many of the slaves were purchased right off the ships by plantation owners. Others were taken to auction houses where they were sold to the highest bidder. South Carolina slaves worked on indigo (a clothing dye) and rice plantations. In North Carolina, slaves worked mainly on the tobacco plantations and in the lumber business.

# Slave Codes

As more and more slaves came into North Carolina, the rules regarding slavery changed. The white settlers grew fearful that the increasing slave population might revolt and overthrow the white masters. A serious revolt had occurred in South Carolina in 1731 on the Stono River, where white settlers had been killed.

After this rebellion, North Carolina passed a series of slave codes that restricted the lives of the slaves. Slaves were to remain the property of their masters for life. They were not allowed to learn to read or write. Slave owners believed that this restriction would prevent the slaves on neighboring plantations from communicating with each other. If they could not contact each other, then they would not be able to plan a rebellion. Slaves were not allowed to travel without special passes signed by their masters. They were not allowed to gather for meetings or celebrations. Plantation owners could treat their slaves very harshly with no worry of being punished.

*Slave women worked alongside the men, toiling at whatever job was required by the master.*

*Plantations were large farms, worked by slaves, who tended crops from sunrise to sunset, six days a week.*

# Plantation Life

North Carolina had only a few large plantations. Most of those were located on the Cape Fear River. One plantation owner named Thomas Pollock owned 40,000 acres (16,000 hectares) and one hundred slaves.

On large plantations, slaves were often supervised by overseers. These were usually white men who watched over the day-to-day work of the slaves. Some overseers were very cruel. An overseer could whip or even kill slaves if he didn't think they were working hard enough. But many plantation owners felt a responsibility to care for their slaves, providing them with food, housing, and medical care. Nevertheless, slave owners did not act out of kindness. They were simply protecting their **investment**. Slaves were expensive property to buy. Their owners, or masters, wanted to make sure that the slaves were kept healthy enough to work.

Most plantation owners in North Carolina owned fewer than twenty slaves. The slaves lived in separate cabins near the owner's home. These cabins usually had one room, with a window and a fireplace. During the eighteenth century, some slaves were permitted to keep their own gardens in which they grew vegetables. Some may have grown a little tobacco, which they were then allowed to sell. A few slaves used the money they saved to buy their freedom. Others were freed when their masters died through instructions left in their masters' wills.

# Working in the Fields

Slaves were expected to work six days a week, or seven during harvest time. Wheat was planted in the fall and spring. Flax was planted in March and harvested in May. Tobacco seedlings were planted in May. One historian described how the slaves worked to grow tobacco:

*Slaves working with hoes formed little hills six to nine feet apart. Once the [tobacco] plants reached a height of one foot they had to be pruned, topped, and the bottom leaves cut off. Twice a week thereafter suckers had to be removed, the hills weeded, and the plant carefully gone over for worms. When the tobacco leaves began to brown in the late summer or early fall, they were cut and piled in stacks and then taken to a shed where they hung for about a month. After being stacked in piles again, this time for one to two weeks, the leaves were finally packed into [barrels].*

When slaves were not planting or harvesting crops, they might be busy cutting trees for lumber or preparing tar and pitch for export. Some slaves learned to be carpenters,

*A slave might work as a grave digger if that service was needed by the plantation owner.*

blacksmiths, **coopers,** or shoemakers. Others were trained as servants to work in the master's home, cooking, cleaning, or caring for the master's children. If there was not enough work for all the slaves on a plantation, they might be hired out to other estates. While slaves were permitted to keep some of the money they earned by being hired out, the rest was paid to their masters.

*Slave children lived with their families until they were old enough to work or be sold to another owner.*

# Slave Culture

Slaves tried hard to hold onto their African traditions and way of life. They danced and sang traditional African songs. They played African instruments such as the drum and the *molo*, which was similar to a banjo. Slaves also continued to use their African language, mixed with English words.

The naming ceremony for a newborn baby was an important African tradition. The slaves gathered together to celebrate the naming of a child by its parents. The parents might select an African name to remember a dead relative or the name of the day on which the child was born. Slaves kept these true names, although their white masters called them by different ones. Favorite names among the plantation owners for their slaves were Ben and Flora. These names may have sounded like the slaves' African names, which were too difficult for the white plantation owners to pronounce.

Slaves also followed the religious beliefs brought from their homelands. Africans believed that people's spirits remained in the world after their deaths. Unless a proper burial ceremony was performed, these spirits would haunt the living.

Among the slaves, a local medicine man held special power. Slaves believed that illness or misfortune was caused by a curse from another person. The medicine man knew how to remove this curse and also how to use herbs or roots to cure illness.

Family life on the plantations was very important to the slaves, since they had lost all contact with their own families in Africa. Keeping family traditions was very difficult. Plantation owners regularly broke up families by selling off one member while keeping the rest. A visitor to North Carolina named Johann David Schoepf reported that

> *often the husband is snatched from his wife,*
> *the children from their mother, if this*
> *better answers the purpose of buyer or seller,*
> *and no heed is given the doleful prayers with*
> *which they seek to prevent a separation.*

## Slave Resistance

Some slaves tried to break free from their owners by running away. Some who had been sold tried to rejoin their families. Others fled westward to the frontier. There, African-Americans could live in freedom, since the small farmers in the west did not keep slaves.

Some slaves headed north to a large, marshy, heavily wooded area called the Great Dismal Swamp. This region stretched from southern Virginia into North Carolina. Slaves could easily hide from their masters in the swamp. Some lived in the Dismal Swamp for years, hunting wildlife to feed themselves and avoiding capture.

Even slaves who remained on plantations found ways to resist their masters. They worked slowly or pretended not to understand what they were supposed to do. Some slaves destroyed tools and crops. Even though some slaves caused trouble, plantation owners continued to import them into North Carolina in growing numbers.

Settlers also continued to move to North Carolina. The population grew to 80,000 by the 1750s. But by then the safety of the plantation owners, settlers, and slaves was threatened. A series of colonial wars between Great Britain and its longtime enemies, the French and Spanish, was about to begin. These wars would reshape life in North Carolina and all of North America.

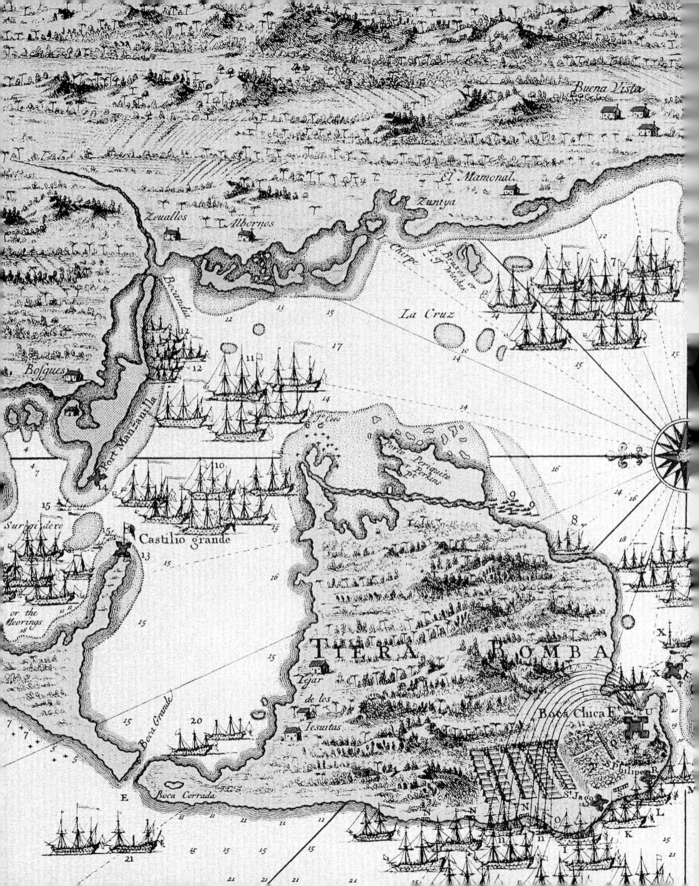

Buena Vista

El Mamonal

Zuniya

Churpe

Zeuallos

Albornos

L. Brazos or L. of Watches

Bocachita

La Cruz

Bofques

Port Manzanilla

Tocco

Porto Peroquito or Perkins P.te

11

17

12

14

7

Surgidero

Castilio grande

13

Tiera Bomba

Tejar de los Jesuitas

Boca Grande

Boca Chica

St Philipe

St Jago

Boca Corrada

8

9

10

12

20

21

or the Moorings

16

15

14

18

# CHAPTER SIX

# Warfare Shapes North Carolina

## Fighting the Spanish

During the eighteenth century, troops from North Carolina fought in several wars between England, France, and Spain. These countries were fighting for control of the New World. Wars were fought in North America, South America, and the Caribbean.

In 1740, four companies of the North Carolina militia sailed to Cartagena to fight for Britain against the Spanish. Cartagena was a settlement on the northern coast of South America that was controlled by the Spanish. It was a long journey for the militiamen, most of whom had never left North Carolina before. But North Carolina was part of the British Empire. England was in a war with Spain for control

*This map of Cartagena shows the forts and ships surrounding the harbor.*

of rich colonies in the New World. England expected the colonists to help in the fight.

The North Carolina troops first sailed to the British colony of Jamaica, where they joined 12,000 English soldiers commanded by General Thomas Wentworth. From Jamaica, they journeyed to Cartagena. The English planned to surprise the enemy and attack at night, but the assault was delayed. The Spanish got word of the attack and were ready for it. As the English and colonial troops tried to climb the walls of the Spanish settlement, they were slaughtered by gunfire. One of the North Carolina companies lost 75 percent of its soldiers.

While the English were being defeated at Cartagena, Spanish ships sailed north and began to attack the North Carolina coast. The Spanish established a base at Ocracoke Island and started attacking colonial merchant ships. The Spanish were beaten back by the English, but the war between Spain and England grew. France joined the Spanish, and Austria sided with England.

The Spanish continued their raids along the North Carolina coast. They attacked the port of Beaufort and entered Brunswick before being driven out by the local militia. The conflict that took place in North America from 1744 to 1748 was known as King George's War, for the English monarch, George II.

*British troops gathered in North Carolina to fight the Spanish and French during King George's War.*

# The French and Indian War

The peace treaty ending King George's War lasted only a few years. Soon after, France and England began fighting again. They battled for control of North America. The French had colonies in present-day Canada, which was called New France. France also owned Louisiana along the

*The French defeated George Washington's small army at Great Meadows in western Pennsylvania.*

Mississippi River, with a population of 80,000. The number of English settlers in North America had reached 1.25 million. However, French traders had moved into the Great Lakes and the Mississippi River valley. The traders had become friends with the powerful native tribes in the region.

In 1753, the French governor in New France, Marquis Duquesne, began to take control of the Ohio River valley. His plan was to link the two territories controlled by the French—Canada and Louisiana. French soldiers built a series of forts south from Lake Erie.

The leaders of North Carolina didn't want the French to control the Ohio Valley. French rule there would prevent English farmers from traveling westward to settle new land. The royal governor of North Carolina, Matthew Rowan, asked the colonial assembly to act. "You know too well gentlemen the Importance of the Western Territory to these Colonies to sit still and tamely see a formidable foreign Power possess themselves of it," Rowan said. The assembly voted to raise troops that would defend the western frontier of North Carolina from the French. But the vote came too late. War had already broken out to the north.

In July 1754, Lieutenant George Washington and a small army had been defeated by the French at Great Meadows in western Pennsylvania. France now controlled the entire Ohio Valley. The Indian tribes who lived there were ready to fight for the French.

# Struggle for Victory

Early in 1755, England sent General Edward Braddock and an army of troops to North America to drive back the French. Joining the English soldiers were colonial militia from Virginia, Maryland, and North Carolina. They began constructing a road westward through the forests. The army needed to reach the French at Fort Duquesne in western Pennsylvania.

In order to move faster, Braddock decided to split his 2,200 troops. Some remained behind with the slow-moving supply wagons. Others marched more rapidly toward the fort. By early July, the army was within 10 miles (16 kilometers) of its target. It had not met up with any French troops. The troops thought they would easily reach the French fort and begin their attack.

At Fort Duquesne, the French commander, Captain Claude-Pierre Contrecoeur, had only a few hundred French soldiers. But he also had several hundred Indians camped outside the fort, ready to fight for the French. On July 9, Contrecoeur sent a force of 900 men to ambush the English. The North Carolina militiamen had been sent off on a scouting expedition. They missed the terrible fighting on the Monongahela River. The bloody battle became known as Braddock's Defeat.

# Braddock's Defeat

On the way to Fort Duquesne, General Braddock had sent scouts into the woods in case the enemy should try to take his troops by surprise. But the French and Indians approached from the front. They were spotted by British soldiers just after the French and Indian force crossed the Monongahela River. The British immediately fired and killed the French leader, Daniel Lienard de Beaujeu.

The Indians fighting for the French scattered into the woods and hid behind trees. They returned fire against the English. To defend themselves, the British troops formed lines, as they had always done on the open battlefields of Europe. But here in the woods, they became easy targets for the Indians.

The colonial militia tried to hide behind rocks and trees to fight like the Indians. General Braddock insisted that his men stand in the open and keep firing. He was convinced that they would eventually win the battle. However, as one soldier put it, "The French and Indians crept about in small Parties so that the Fire was quite round us, and in all the Time I never saw one, Nor could I...find any one who saw ten together." Braddock kept riding among his men, encouraging them to fight. Eventually, he was hit by enemy fire and died. Afterward, the British and colonial troops fled from the battlefield.

The English defeat caused trouble for the Virginia and North Carolina frontier. The Indians realized that the British army was no longer there to defend colonists. Natives attacked English settlements in North Carolina, burning farmhouses and killing many settlers.

*The English battle strategy was no match for the French and Indians, who used the forest to hide in small groups and launch surprise attacks.*

# British Triumph

In 1758, the British launched a new assault against Fort Duquesne, led by General John Forbes. Soldiers from the North Carolina militia fought alongside British soldiers. During the summer of 1758, Forbes's men built a road westward from Pennsylvania toward the Ohio River. This route was much shorter than the one Braddock had used in 1755.

At the same time, conditions at Fort Duquesne had grown worse for the French. British victories in other parts of the region had cut off their supplies. Then the British signed a treaty with France's Indian allies. The British promised to protect Indian hunting grounds if the Indian tribes would abandon their support for the French.

The French decided to blow up Fort Duquesne and retreat to the north. Reaching the fort, the English troops saw the mighty stronghold explode into flames. The English later built Fort Pitt on the spot where the French fort had stood and where the city of Pittsburgh, Pennsylvania, now stands.

One year later, the British captured the French headquarters at Quebec on the St. Lawrence River. In 1760, Montreal, another French stronghold on the St. Lawrence River, fell to the English. The French and Indian War ended. England took control of the French lands in New France and renamed them Canada.

# War Against the Cherokee

When the French and Indian War ended, a new conflict broke out. This time the English battled the Cherokee Indians. The fighting began in South Carolina but moved into North Carolina. The Cherokee of Carolina were among the Indians who had supported General Forbes's campaign. On their way home from battle, some of the Cherokee were accused of stealing horses from Virginia settlers. The natives were attacked by the settlers, and at least thirty Indians were killed.

*The Cherokee fought bitterly against settlers who moved onto sacred native hunting grounds.*

When the Cherokee reached their homes, they found that the settlers of South Carolina had moved onto Indian hunting grounds. War broke out between the Indians and the South Carolina militia in 1759. The fighting soon spread to North Carolina.

In 1761, English troops arrived. They destroyed the Cherokee's villages and burned their cornfields. As a result, the Cherokee agreed to a peace treaty.

The defeat of the French and the Cherokee opened up the western frontier for North Carolina settlers. These new settlements, however, would bring new problems for the colonists. The next and bloodiest fight—against the British—would soon begin.

# CHAPTER SEVEN

# The Coming of Revolution

## West vs. East

Following the French and Indian War and the battles with the Cherokee, North Carolina's backcountry became a safer place to live. More settlers moved into this region. As the population grew, the settlers wanted more power in the colony's government. Instead of fighting the French or Indians, North Carolina's citizens began to squabble with each other over political control of the colony.

Edmund Fanning was considered one of the most powerful politicians in North Carolina in the 1760s. He was a judge and a friend of William Tryon, the colony's governor. He was also a member of the assembly that represented the county of Orange. But Fanning was not well liked by the

*Warring with the Indians was soon to give way to the War of Independence.*

settlers living in Orange. The settlers believed he was dishonest. One of the residents even composed a poem about him:

> When Fanning first to Orange came
> He look'd both pale and wan:
> An old patch'd coat upon his back,
> An old mare he rode on.
> Both man and mare wa'nt [weren't]
> worth five pounds
> As I've been often told;
> But by his civil robberies,
> He's laced his coat with gold.

This poem about Fanning told of an argument within North Carolina. The powerful eastern counties near the coast did not get along with the western counties of the colony. The governor lived in the east, and the colonial assembly met there. The governor appointed the judges, like Fanning. The governor also appointed the justices of the peace, who were the most powerful officials in each county. Representatives to the assembly were elected from each county. The more counties a section of the colony had, the more representatives it could elect.

## Governor William Tryon

William Tryon was born in 1729 in Surrey, a village in southern England. He was one of seven children, who grew up on a large estate called Norbury Park. At age twenty-one, Tryon joined the army. While serving in the military in 1757, he married Margaret Wake, the daughter of a wealthy merchant. The following year, Tryon fought in a bloody battle in the French and Indian War. He helped his men make a successful retreat.

After the war ended, Tryon grew bored serving in the army. He became lieutenant governor of North Carolina in 1764. Tryon and his wife moved to North Carolina and lived in Wilmington. During his first year in the colony, he traveled around to learn as much as he could about North Carolina. Along the way, he stopped at large plantations where the owners entertained him. In 1765, the governor, Arthur Dobbs, retired, and Tryon was appointed to take his place. Tryon later served as governor of New York.

Many people were moving into the backcountry. But the assembly did not want to create new counties there. The eastern counties were greater in number. They were thus able to control the assembly and hold most of the power in the colony. In 1766, the assembly decided that the capital of North Carolina should be located at New Bern, near the east coast. The legislators also decided to build a palace for Governor Tryon.

*Governor Tryon was forced to march against the Regulators when they used violent methods to protest government policies.*

This decision made the people in the backcountry very angry. They were upset that their taxes were going to be used to build a palace for the wealthy governor. As one critic put it, "Not one man in twenty of the four most populous counties [in the backcountry] will ever see this famous house when built."

# The Regulators

The backcountry settlers decided that they didn't want to have their lives controlled by the powerful eastern counties. The unhappy western settlers wanted to control, or regulate, their own local affairs. In 1768, they formed a group called the Regulators.

The Regulators complained that the eastern leaders were growing rich by stealing their tax money. One of their main targets was Fanning. A group of Regulators attacked Fanning's house in Hillsboro, North Carolina. The Regulators also wrote and distributed pamphlets complaining about political corruption.

Governor Tryon ordered the Regulators to stop their protests, but they ignored him. In 1768, the Regulators attacked the court in Hillsboro. Fanning was there that day. He was grabbed by a group of Regulators, carried outside, and severely beaten.

Again, Governor Tryon ordered the Regulators to stop their activities, but they refused. Finally, in 1771, the governor and the North Carolina militia marched against them. During a battle in the town of Alamance, Tryon's soldiers defeated a Regulator army of about 2,000 men. Regulator leaders were captured, tried, and hanged. The Regulator movement came to an end.

## Conflict With Great Britain

While North Carolina settlers were battling for power against their governor, another struggle had begun. This conflict between the American colonies and Great Britain would soon erupt into war.

Although England had triumphed in the French and Indian War, France and Spain still controlled colonies in Louisiana and Florida. There were also powerful Indian tribes living in the west along the Ohio and Mississippi rivers. British leaders believed that they still needed to defend their American colonies against possible attacks. They also believed that the colonies should help pay the cost of this defense.

During the 1760s, Parliament passed a series of taxes that the colonists had to pay. The colonists strongly protested each tax. The colonists did not want to pay taxes to England when they had no voice in the English government. Their motto became "Taxation without representation is **tyranny**!"

*Colonists protested the many taxes England forced upon the colonies.*

The Stamp Act of 1765 required the colonists to buy stamps for any printed papers. These included legal documents, pamphlets, and papers that allowed ships to enter colonial harbors. The colonists could not do business without the stamps.

Many of the colonists refused to buy the stamps. A group of North Carolina's business leaders formed a protest group called the Sons of Liberty. Similar groups were springing up in other colonies, too, as protests against the Stamp Act grew. In Wilmington, North Carolina, several hundred people surrounded the house of Dr. William Houston. Houston had been appointed to collect the taxes. He was so frightened by the crowd that he promised not to carry out his duties. The colonists also stopped importing goods from England as a protest against the Stamp Act. English merchants lost so much money that they made Parliament repeal the Stamp Act in 1766.

One year later, however, Parliament passed the Townshend Acts. These new laws called for a series of taxes on imported items, such as glass, paint, and paper. The North Carolina Assembly spoke out against these new taxes, arguing that they were, again, taxation without representation. Joining other colonies, North Carolina legislators decided once again to stop importing English goods. Backing down again, Parliament repealed the Townshend Acts in 1770.

# The Coming of Revolution

In 1773, Britain imposed the Tea Act. This act allowed the British East India Company to sell tea to the colonists without paying a tax. The company's tea was therefore cheaper than the tea of colonial merchants. The merchants knew that no one would buy tea from them if it was more expensive. Protests against the tea tax spread throughout the North American colonies. In Boston, Massachusetts, a group of Patriots (those in favor of breaking away from England) disguised as Indians threw the tea from an English ship into Boston Harbor. This event became known as the Boston Tea Party. The English government, furious with the colonists, closed the port of Boston in 1774.

The colonists held a meeting to discuss the unfair taxes and come up with a plan of action. The meeting was called the First Continental Congress. It took place in Philadelphia, Pennsylvania, in 1774. North Carolina did not send any representatives to the meeting because Governor Josiah Martin refused to select them.

North Carolina legislators held their own meeting, called the First Provincial Congress, in August 1774. Representatives there strongly opposed the taxes being passed by Parliament. At the Second Provincial Congress, held in 1775, North Carolina selected people to attend another meeting of all of the colonies. This was called the Second Continental Congress.

## The Edenton Tea Party

In 1774, in Edenton, North Carolina, more than fifty colonial women pledged their support for America's defense of its freedom. Led by Mrs. Penelope Barker, they announced, "We the Ladys of Edenton, do hereby solemnly engage not to conform to the Pernicious Custom of Drinking Tea." Furthermore, they added, "We, the aforesaid Ladys will not promote ye wear of any manufacturer from England until such time that all acts which tend to enslave our Native country shall be repealed." Historians believe that the so-called Edenton Tea Party was the first time women in the American colonies took an active role in politics.

# War Begins in North Carolina

Governor Martin opposed the actions of the North Carolina Provincial Congress. He wanted the British to control the colony, but the colonists didn't listen to him. During 1774 and 1775, colonists set up groups called safety committees in North Carolina towns. These groups were intended to prepare the colonists to defend themselves in case of war.

*The First Provincial Congress was an official gathering of North Carolina lawmakers who strongly opposed British taxes.*

In Mecklenburg County, the safety committee declared that the settlers there were "a free and independent people." These words are known as the Mecklenburg Declaration of Independence. Governor Martin was angry at the committee and its declaration. He wrote that "they surpass all the horrid and treasonable publications that the inflammatory spirits of this Continent have yet produced." As the colonists' protests began to grow, the governor feared for his safety. Martin placed cannons outside his palace to protect himself. The guns were quickly stolen by North Carolina Patriots.

Governor Martin left his palace at New Bern and fled to the coast in late May 1775. He hid on a British warship. With the governor gone, North Carolina created a new government. In August, the Third Provincial Congress met at Hillsboro. Lawmakers asked for a Provincial Council to be elected to run the colony. All colonists were urged to obtain guns and prepare for the coming fight. The new government also decided to raise troops to defend the colony.

By this time, battles had already broken out in Massachusetts. In April 1775, colonial militia fought British soldiers at Lexington and Concord. Troops from several colonies then battled the British army outside of Boston. The Revolutionary War had begun. North Carolina would soon play a major role in the struggle for a new nation.

# CHAPTER EIGHT

# Independence and Statehood

## The Revolution in North Carolina

The Battle of Moore's Creek Bridge marked the start of the Revolutionary War in North Carolina. In the early morning hours of February 27, 1776, a small army gathered together. These soldiers were **Tories**. The soldiers advanced toward Moore's Creek Bridge outside of Wilmington.

The Tories, many of them Scots, were under the command of Lieutenant Colonel Donald McLeod. Governor Josiah Martin had called on the Tories to defeat "a most daring, horrid, and unnatural Rebellion." Martin had also convinced the British government to send more troops into North Carolina to support the Tories.

*When the British army moved into the southern colonies, North Carolina became the site of many important Revolutionary War battles.*

Defending the bridge was a force of about 1,000 colonial militiamen, commanded by Colonel Richard Caswell. These Patriots had removed the wooden planks from the bridge. They had put grease all over the bridge's frame, making it difficult for the Scots to cross. Caswell's men also dug trenches near the creek where they hid, preparing to fire at the enemy.

About an hour before sunrise, the Scots advanced on the bridge with their bagpipes playing. As they attempted to cross, they were met with gunfire from Caswell's militia. Thirty of the Scots were killed. Many more were wounded. The Tories ran from the battlefield.

The Battle of Moore's Creek Bridge was called "the Lexington and Concord of the South." The Patriot victory saved North Carolina from British invasion. It made the British generals who were supposed to invade North Carolina change their minds. The British army moved elsewhere.

In April 1776, North Carolina became the first colony to instruct its delegates to vote for independence at the Second Continental Congress in Philadelphia. The national Declaration of Independence was signed in July. The declaration announced that the colonies were no longer under British control. North Carolina immediately supported it. The colony began calling itself the state of North Carolina.

*This is an image of the Declaration of Independence, which was signed by North Carolina and twelve other states in 1776.*

A local militia was raised to defend the state's borders. Other North Carolina citizens joined the Continental American army under the command of General George Washington.

During 1777, North Carolina militia participated in the battles around Philadelphia. North Carolina also sent out privateers to attack English merchant ships supplying the British army.

# War in the South

The battle for the southern colonies began in 1778. The British invaded the South, capturing Savannah, Georgia. They later captured Charles Town, South Carolina. From Charles Town, the British moved inland and took control of the entire state.

British general Charles Cornwallis decided to advance into North Carolina. His troops were joined by a force of Tories commanded by Major Patrick Ferguson. Ferguson led his men to King's Mountain, just south of the North Carolina border. There, in early October 1780, he was attacked by Patriot militia, including men from North Carolina. Surrounding Ferguson's troops, the militia killed him and defeated his army. Afraid of defeat, Cornwallis immediately left North Carolina, retreating southward.

American forces received a new commander, General Nathanael Greene. He was one of George Washington's most trusted officers. Major General Greene had shown that he was a brilliant military commander. He had helped Washington during important battles in New Jersey and New York. Greene took command of the Patriot army in the late fall of 1780.

Greene immediately decided to split his forces. He sent part of his army westward under the leadership of General

## Colonial Muskets

Muskets are long-barreled guns that are fired from the shoulder. They are similar to modern rifles but are loaded from the front of the barrel, one shot at a time.

Most men owned at least one musket for hunting. Young men, and many women, learned to load and fire a musket as children.

Reloading a musket required many steps. First a measured amount of gunpowder was poured into the barrel. Next cloth was inserted, followed by a round ball or bullet. Then the gunpowder, cloth, and ball were pushed into the barrel using a long rod.

Before the gun could be fired, gunpowder was put into a small

*A colonial militiaman pours gunpowder into the trigger pan of his musket.*

pan near the trigger. The hammer was pulled back and released by pulling the trigger. When the hammer hit the powder, it caused a spark that fired the gun.

Even with all these steps, most colonial soldiers could fire three or four shots per minute.

Daniel Morgan. Greene hoped that Cornwallis would also split his army. Greene wanted part of the British army to chase Morgan. This would give the Patriots a better chance to defeat the British.

Cornwallis did just as Greene had hoped. He sent half of his army, led by Colonel Banastre Tarleton, to follow

*North Carolina militiamen were on the front lines at the Battle of Cowpens in South Carolina.*

Morgan. The two small armies each numbered about 1,000 men. They met in January 1781 at the Battle of Cowpens, South Carolina. Morgan put the North Carolina militia in the front line. He told them to take a few shots and then retreat. As Tarleton's men chased the North Carolina militia, the rest of Morgan's army hit the British with heavy musket fire. Tarleton's army was smashed. Tarleton was one of the few men to escape from the battlefield alive.

General Greene brought his army back together with Morgan's forces. Greene hoped Cornwallis would chase after him through North Carolina. If Cornwallis did this, the British army would end up many miles from its supply base in Charles Town. At the right moment, Greene wanted to turn around and attack Cornwallis. He believed his plan would destroy the British army.

General Cornwallis decided that he could not allow Greene to escape. He moved his forces into North Carolina, hoping to catch the American army. Greene's troops defended themselves at the town of Guilford courthouse, North Carolina. He formed his army into three lines. The North Carolina militiamen were in front. Greene told them, "Two rounds, my boys, and then you may fall back." Behind the North Carolina militia, Greene set up another line of colonial militia. On a hillside near the courthouse, he placed the experienced Continental soldiers.

Cornwallis began his attack on the Americans early in the afternoon of March 15, 1781. The North Carolina militia carried out its orders, firing two rounds and then quickly retreating from the battlefield. The British kept advancing and pushed back the Americans' second line of defense.

At this point, Cornwallis made the unusual decision to fire his cannons into the battle. He killed some of the Americans, but he also took the lives of some of his own troops. Greene ordered a retreat in order to safeguard the rest of his soldiers.

Cornwallis had won a victory, but at a great cost. Many of his soldiers were dead. He had few supplies, and he was many miles away from a British supply base. As one British officer wrote,

*I never did and I never shall experience*
*two such days and nights as those immediately*
*after the battle. We remained on the very*
*ground on which it had been fought,*
*covered with dead, with dying, and*
*hundreds of wounded.... A violent and*
*constant rain that lasted over forty hours*
*made it equally impracticable to remove*
*or administer the smallest comfort to*
*many of the wounded. In this situation*
*we expected every moment to be attacked.*

Cornwallis headed for Virginia to get supplies from British warships. But when his forces reached Yorktown, Virginia, they were trapped by American troops. The Americans forced Cornwallis to surrender on October 19, 1781. It was the last major battle of the Revolutionary War.

# A New Government

Now that the war was over, the new United States of America needed a new government. During the Revolutionary War, the American states had been governed by a document called the Articles of Confederation. Under these laws, the central government remained very weak. The states did not want to be controlled by a strong central government, as they had been under British rule.

Under the Articles of Confederation, individual states were able to trade with foreign countries. This made it very difficult for any European country to make a trade agreement with the entire United States of America. The states were not required to pay any taxes. The central government did not even have the power to raise an army to defend the new nation.

The weakness of the government under the Articles of Confederation convinced the colonies that they needed new laws to fit the needs of the new nation. To write these new laws, American leaders met in Philadelphia in 1787. North Carolina sent a group of five men to the Philadelphia convention. William Davie, William Blount, and Richard Spaight were successful plantation owners. All three owned slaves. A lawyer named Alexander Martin and Hugh Williamson, a doctor and merchant, were also part of the North Carolina delegation.

At the convention, the delegates decided that they would create a totally new form of government. The laws establishing the new government would be written in a document called the Constitution. This was not an easy task. Arguments occurred between the small and large states. North Carolina was one of the largest states, with a population of about 350,000.

Some of the delegates, including William Davie, developed a compromise. It called for a Congress with two parts. One, the House of Representatives, would be based on population. This rule gave the large states an advantage, because they would have more elected representatives than the smaller states. The other part of Congress, the Senate, would have the same number of elected senators from each state. This arrangement made sure that the rights of the small states were protected.

The North Carolina delegates wanted a section of the Constitution that protected the Southern slave states. The number of representatives in Congress would be based on white voters, as well as black slaves. Each slave would count as just three-fifths of a person in this process. In addition, the slave trade would be allowed to continue until 1808. Thus, plantation owners in North Carolina and the rest of the South could bring in additional slaves to work in their fields. After that date, no slaves could be legally imported into the United States.

*Colonists gather to hear news of the new government being formed following the end of the Revolutionary War.*

# Approving the Constitution

In July 1788, North Carolina's delegates met at Hillsboro to vote on the new Constitution. By this time, ten other states had already approved it. The Constitution only needed the approval of nine states for it to become the official law of the new country. But the leaders of the country wanted the support of all the states so the government would run smoothly.

At first, the North Carolina delegates refused to ratify the Constitution. They felt that amendments, or additions, were necessary to protect the freedom of the American people. Eventually, a list of laws called the Bill of Rights was proposed. North Carolina approved the Constitution in 1789. It became the twelfth state to enter the new United States.

The leaders of North Carolina now turned their attention to the location of their new state capital. In the past, the assembly had met in different towns, including Hillsboro and New Bern. Westerners wanted the capital to be located near the center of the state, so that all regions could be equally represented. Eventually, a new town in central North Carolina was selected for the capital. The town was named Raleigh.

The history of colonial North Carolina was complete. The earliest settlements had been founded under the direction of Sir Walter Raleigh. Now, the new state had a capital city named after the great man.

# Recipe
## Short'nin' Bread

The Scotch-Irish settlers who moved to the North Carolina backcountry brought a recipe with them for a cake that became known as shortening bread. The name was pronounced *short'nin'* in the southern colonies. This was a treat enjoyed by both rich and poor southern households. Short'nin bread was so popular that a song was written about it.

*Three little children, lying in bed,*
*Two were sick and the other most dead!*
*Sent for the doctor, the doctor said:*
*"Feed these children on short'nin' bread."*

*Mamma's little baby loves short'nin', short'nin',*
*Mamma's little baby loves short'nin' bread.*
*Mamma's little baby loves short'nin', short'nin',*
*Mamma's little baby loves short'nin' bread.*

*2 cups sifted flour*
*1/2 teaspoon salt*
*1/2 cup light*
*brown sugar*
*1 cup chilled sweet*
*(unsalted) butter*

- Set oven temperature to 350 degrees.
- Mix the flour and salt in a large bowl.
- Add the brown sugar to the flour and salt mixture.
- Mix until the sugar is free of lumps.
- Cut the butter into chunks, and add it to the mixture.
- Using a pastry blender, work the butter into the flour mixture until the butter chunks are about the size of peas.

- Work the mixture with your hands until it forms a smooth dough.
- Press the dough into a buttered 9-inch-square baking pan.
- Spread the dough evenly in the pan.
- Use a fork to prick holes in the surface of the dough.
- Bake for 20 to 25 minutes or until light brown.
- Remove the pan from the oven and let cool.
- Cut into squares.

*This activity should be done with adult supervision*

# Activity
## Pomander Ball

Colonial homes were often stuffy. Doors and windows were kept closed during the winter to keep the heat inside. Even in summer, there were no fans or air conditioning to make the air fresh. Odors from cooking and people who seldom bathed could make the house smell pretty bad.

Colonial women made a simple air freshener from apples, cloves, and cinnamon. It was called a pomander ball. You can make one to freshen up your school locker or room at home. Colonial women even carried small pomander balls in their handbags or handkerchiefs so they could sniff the pleasant smell.

### *Procedure*

*An apple or orange • Cloves Cinnamon powder • Bowl • Fork or toothpick • Plastic net or cheesecloth String or yarn • Ribbon*

- Make holes in the fruit with the fork or toothpick.
- Insert cloves in the holes.
- Cover the entire fruit with cloves.
- Empty the cinnamon into the bowl. Roll the clove-covered fruit in it until the fruit is covered with cinnamon.
- Place the fruit in the net or wrap it in the cheesecloth.
- Tie the top of the net or cheesecloth with the string or yarn.
- Hang the fruit in a cool, dry place for several days until the fruit has dried.
- When the fruit has dried, take the pomander ball out of the net or cheesecloth.
- Tie the ribbon around the pomander ball so it can be suspended from above.
- Place the pomander ball in your locker, room, or closet and enjoy the sweet smell.

*This activity should be done with adult supervision.*

# North Carolina
# Time Line

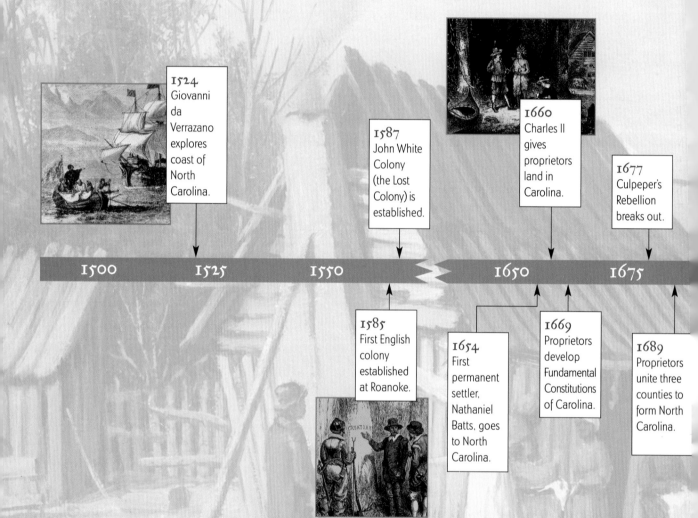

**1524** Giovanni da Verrazano explores coast of North Carolina.

**1587** John White Colony (the Lost Colony) is established.

**1660** Charles II gives proprietors land in Carolina.

**1677** Culpeper's Rebellion breaks out.

**1500**     **1525**     **1550**     **1650**     **1675**

**1585** First English colony established at Roanoke.

**1654** First permanent settler, Nathaniel Batts, goes to North Carolina.

**1669** Proprietors develop Fundamental Constitutions of Carolina.

**1689** Proprietors unite three counties to form North Carolina.

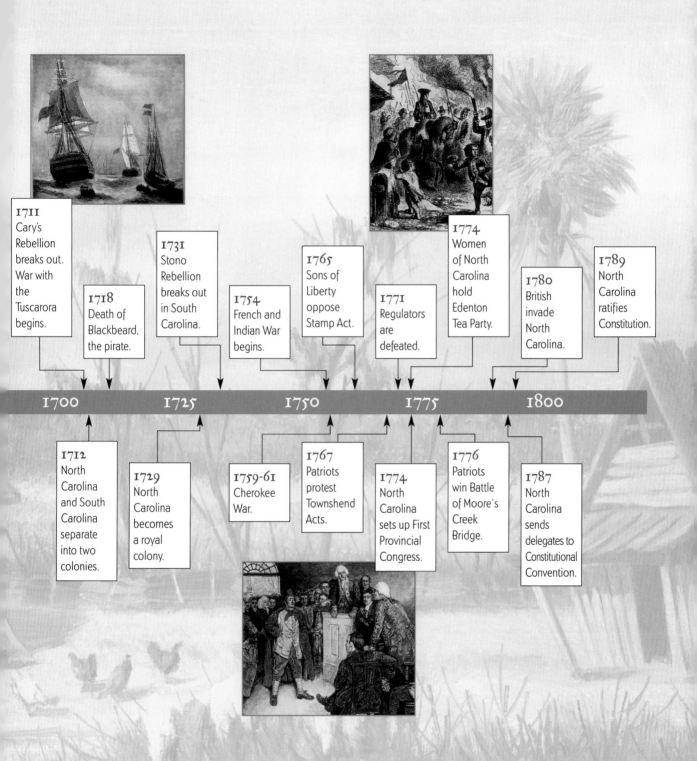

**1711**
Cary's Rebellion breaks out. War with the Tuscarora begins.

**1718**
Death of Blackbeard, the pirate.

**1731**
Stono Rebellion breaks out in South Carolina.

**1754**
French and Indian War begins.

**1765**
Sons of Liberty oppose Stamp Act.

**1771**
Regulators are defeated.

**1774**
Women of North Carolina hold Edenton Tea Party.

**1780**
British invade North Carolina.

**1789**
North Carolina ratifies Constitution.

**1700**   **1725**   **1750**   **1775**   **1800**

**1712**
North Carolina and South Carolina separate into two colonies.

**1729**
North Carolina becomes a royal colony.

**1759-61**
Cherokee War.

**1767**
Patriots protest Townshend Acts.

**1774**
North Carolina sets up First Provincial Congress.

**1776**
Patriots win Battle of Moore's Creek Bridge.

**1787**
North Carolina sends delegates to Constitutional Convention.

119

# Further Reading

Hawke, David. *Everyday Life in Early America.* New York: Harper and Row, 1988.

Kent, Deborah. *How We Lived in the Southern Colonies.* New York: Marshall Cavendish, 2000.

Leckie, Robert. *A Few Acres of Snow: The Saga of the French and Indian Wars.* New York: Wiley, 1999.

Lefler, Hugh, and William Powell. *Colonial North Carolina: A History.* New York: Scribner's, 1973.

Uschan, Michael. *The Thirteen Colonies: North Carolina.* San Diego: Lucent Books, 2002.

Wolf, Stephanie Grauman. *As Various As Their Land: The Everyday Lives of Eighteenth-Century Americans.* New York: HarperCollins, 1993.

# Glossary

abundant  more than enough

bounty  generous or plentiful supply

charter  an official document that details rights
and privileges

cooper  a person skilled in making or repairing barrels

county  territorial division of a region or local government

expedition  a trip or mission undertaken for a specific
reason

hospitality  welcoming or kind treatment

indentured servant  someone who worked for no pay in
exchange for travel to, and housing in, the colonies

investment  an asset; someone or something for which
money exchanged hands

loincloth  a piece of cloth worn around the hips;
also known as a breechcloth

oath  a solemn or sacred promise

palisade  a fence made of logs sharpened at the top that surrounds a town or settlement for protection

parliament  formal assembly of a governing body

privateer  owner of a ship hired by a government to attack and rob enemy ships

proprietor  one of eight men given power by King Charles II of England to run present-day North Carolina, South Carolina, and Georgia

rebellion  revolt or uprising; resistance to those in power

repeal  to undo, cancel, or abolish something, such as a law

spinning  the process of making thread or yarn from raw material such as wool, cotton, or flax

stronghold  fortress; a place that is easily defended against enemies

surplus  left over or an extra amount

surveyor-general person who measures land to determine borders or boundaries

Tory  colonist who remained loyal to Great Britain during the Revolutionary War

tyranny  abusive government power

# Index